Disaster!

The Challenger

The Explosion on Liftoff

by Tom Streissguth

Consultant:
James Gerard
Aerospace Education Specialist
NASA Aerospace Education Services Program

CAPSTONE
HIGH-INTEREST
BOOKS

an imprint of Capstone Press
Mankato, Minnesota

Capstone High-Interest Books are published by Capstone Press
151 Good Counsel Drive, P.O. Box 669, Mankato, Minnesota 56002
http://www.capstone-press.com

Library of Congress Cataloging-in-Publication Data
Streissguth, Thomas, 1958-
    The Challenger: the explosion on liftoff/by Tom Streissguth.
    p. cm.—(Disaster!)
    Summary: Portrays the space shuttle Challenger, the events that led to its
destruction, and the effects of the disaster on the space program.
    Includes bibliographical references and index.
    ISBN 0-7368-1322-5
    1. Challenger (Spacecraft)—Juvenile literature. 2. Space vehicle
accidents—United States. [1. Challenger (Spacecraft) 2. Space shuttles.
3. Space vehicle accidents.] I. Title. II. Disaster! (Capstone High-Interest
Books)
TL867 .S774 2003
363.12'4—dc21   2001008335

Editorial Credits
Matt Doeden, editor; Karen Risch, product planning editor; Kia Adams,
    designer; Jo Miller, photo researcher

Photo Credits
Corbis, 24
George D. Lepp/Corbis, 21
Hulton Archive by Getty Images, 4, 6, 9, 10, 12
NASA, cover, 7, 15, 17, 18, 20, 22, 27

1 2 3 4 5 6 07 06 05 04 03 02

Table of Contents

Features

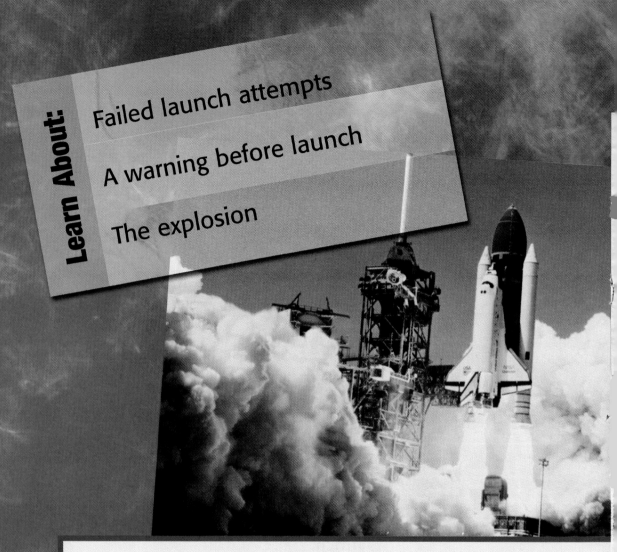

Fast Facts about the *Challenger*

Length of Orbiter: 122 feet (37.2 meters)	**Days in Orbit**: 69
Wingspan of Orbiter: 78 feet (23.8 meters)	**Final Launch**: January 28, 1986
	Altitude at Time of Explosion: 48,000 feet (14,630 meters)
Cost to Build: About $2 billion	**Length of Flight**: 73.1 seconds
First Launch: April 4, 1983	**Crew Members Aboard**: 7
Missions Flown: 10	**Survivors**: 0

The Disaster

On the morning of January 28, 1986, the space shuttle *Challenger* stood on the launch pad at Kennedy Space Center in Florida. Crew members inside the shuttle made their final preparations for the launch. Experts from the National Aeronautics and Space Administration (NASA) made preparations from the space center. Soon, the countdown to launch began.

Launch Delays

NASA officials had planned for *Challenger* to launch on January 23. But the launch date was pushed back because space shuttle *Columbia* had launched only 11 days earlier. NASA officials then planned for a January 25 launch.

NASA prepared *Challenger* for launch several times before January 28.

The *Challenger* crew prepared for the new launch date. But a storm hit *Challenger*'s emergency landing spot in Dakar, Senegal. Because of the storm, *Challenger* could not land if it had problems during launch. Stormy weather in Florida then caused the launch date to be delayed to January 27. Next, a problem with one of *Challenger*'s doors delayed the launch another day.

Some NASA officials were unhappy with all of the delays. They wanted the launch to stay on schedule. They worried about losing money while *Challenger* waited to be launched. They also worried that the delays would make NASA look like it was doing a bad job.

On the morning of January 28, *Challenger*'s launch pad was covered with icicles.

The Decision to Launch

The weather in Florida was unusually cold on the morning of January 28. Icicles covered the launch pad. An engineer from a company called Morton Thiokol called NASA officials early that morning. Morton Thiokol had built *Challenger*'s solid-rocket boosters (SRBs). The engineer told NASA officials that the cold weather could harm the boosters. He asked NASA to delay the launch.

NASA officials had already talked about this problem. They believed that the boosters would work properly even in cold weather. They ignored the engineer's warning and decided to launch.

Liftoff

Challenger began liftoff at 11:38 that morning. Inside the three main engines, liquid hydrogen and liquid oxygen mixed. These two substances explode when they contact each other. A huge cloud of smoke formed from the bottom of the space shuttle. The force of the mixing hydrogen and oxygen pushed the shuttle into the air. Everything appeared to be working perfectly.

In the first seconds after launch, black smoke came from the side of the right SRB. Hot gases escaped through the booster seals, called O-rings. The rubber O-rings were beginning to burn and wear away, but NASA officials did not notice the problem.

At first, *Challenger*'s launch appeared to be going smoothly.

Disaster

Thirty-seven seconds into the flight, the SRBs burned at full power. Almost a minute into the launch, hot gases leaked from the right booster. The gases quickly burst into flame. The flame then spread to the lower part of the external tank. This part of the tank was not built to withstand the flames.

Challenger exploded about 73 seconds after launch.

The flames caused the external tank to leak liquid hydrogen into the air. They also caused the right SRB to break away from the rod that connected it to the tank. The SRB then slammed into the tank. *Challenger* was about 46,000 feet (14,000 meters) above the ground at this time.

More liquid hydrogen and liquid oxygen escaped. The substances mixed and burned out of control. The shuttle exploded 73 seconds into the flight.

A huge ball of flame appeared in the sky. Trails of smoke appeared as the SRBs flew out of control. *Challenger's* crew compartment broke away from the tanks. It continued to rise for a short time, but gravity then pulled it down. The compartment slammed into the Atlantic Ocean.

All seven of *Challenger's* crew members died in the disaster. NASA officials are not certain when they died. Many officials believe the crew died in the explosion. Some people think they might have lived until the crew compartment slammed into the ocean.

History and Design

NASA first began planning space shuttles in the early 1970s. Earlier space vehicles could be used only once. They needed parachutes to fall safely into the ocean. NASA engineers designed space shuttles to land like airplanes. This ability allowed them to go into space many times. NASA sent the first space shuttle, *Columbia*, into space on April 12, 1981.

Parts of the Space Shuttle

The main part of a space shuttle, called the orbiter, includes the crew compartment and the cargo bay. The crew works and lives inside the crew compartment. The cargo bay holds all of the shuttle's large equipment.

Before a launch, NASA officials connect the orbiter to a huge external fuel tank (ET). The ET holds liquid hydrogen and liquid oxygen. These substances are the space shuttle's main source of launch fuel.

Two SRBs also are attached to the ET. These boosters contain chemicals that burn very quickly. The SRBs burn for only about two minutes. They then fall away from the orbiter back to Earth's surface.

When the shuttle is traveling at a speed of about 17,000 miles (27,350 kilometers) per hour, the SRBs fall away. The orbiter reaches an altitude of about 120 miles (193 kilometers) above Earth's surface. The ET then falls away from the orbiter.

In orbit, the pilot steers by using small engines on the front and rear of the shuttle. To land, the orbiter glides safely to the ground without any engine power.

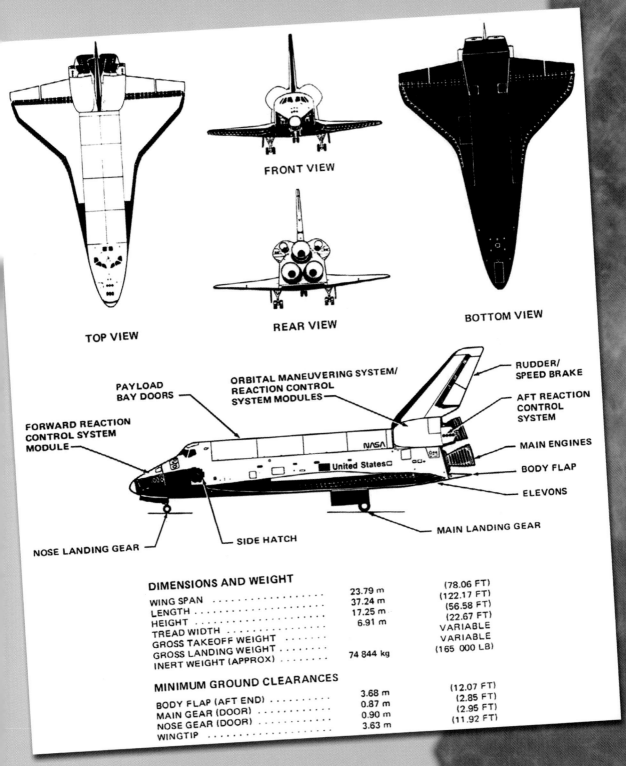

FRONT VIEW

REAR VIEW

BOTTOM VIEW

TOP VIEW

RUDDER/
SPEED BRAKE

PAYLOAD
BAY DOORS

ORBITAL MANEUVERING SYSTEM/
REACTION CONTROL
SYSTEM MODULES

AFT REACTION
CONTROL
SYSTEM

FORWARD REACTION
CONTROL SYSTEM
MODULE

MAIN ENGINES

BODY FLAP

ELEVONS

NOSE LANDING GEAR

SIDE HATCH

MAIN LANDING GEAR

DIMENSIONS AND WEIGHT

WING SPAN	23.79 m	(78.06 FT)
LENGTH	37.24 m	(122.17 FT)
HEIGHT	17.25 m	(56.58 FT)
TREAD WIDTH	6.91 m	(22.67 FT)
GROSS TAKEOFF WEIGHT		VARIABLE
GROSS LANDING WEIGHT		VARIABLE
INERT WEIGHT (APPROX)	74 844 kg	(165 000 LB)

MINIMUM GROUND CLEARANCES

BODY FLAP (AFT END)	3.68 m	(12.07 FT)
MAIN GEAR (DOOR)	0.87 m	(2.85 FT)
NOSE GEAR (DOOR)	0.90 m	(2.95 FT)
WINGTIP	3.63 m	(11.92 FT)

This NASA diagram shows the design
and the specifications of a space shuttle.

Challenger's Crew

Challenger's final launch was supposed to be its 10th trip into space. NASA chose seven people to serve on this mission. Francis Scobee served as the flight commander. As a young man, Scobee enlisted in the U.S. Air Force. There, he learned to fly more than 45 different aircraft.

Challenger's pilot was Michael Smith. During the Vietnam War (1954–1975), he was a pilot in the U.S. Navy. He also had served as a test pilot in the Navy.

Challenger's crew included three mission specialists. Ronald McNair was one of the first three African Americans to join the space program. Judith Resnick became the second U.S. woman in space when she was on the space shuttle *Discovery* in 1984. Ellison Onizuka was a flight test engineer from Hawaii.

Gregory Jarvis was *Challenger*'s payload specialist. Jarvis worked for a company called Hughes Aircraft. His job on *Challenger* was to perform tests on liquid-fueled rockets.

NASA officials wanted to share the space shuttle experience with people who were not scientists or engineers. They wanted to include one other person, called a participant-observer, in *Challenger*'s crew. In 1985, NASA chose teacher Christa McAuliffe of New Hampshire as that crew member. McAuliffe's job was to teach classes from space. NASA planned to send out McAuliffe's lessons by satellite to schools around the United States.

All seven crew members died in the *Challenger* disaster.

Learn About:

- The investigation
- Studying the evidence
- Challenger's O-rings

CHAPTER THREE

What Went Wrong

People around the world quickly learned about the *Challenger* explosion. TV stations ran many stories about the disaster. Newspapers showed large photos of the explosion on their front pages. People wanted to understand how such a disaster could happen.

Pieces of Challenger

Thousands of pieces of *Challenger* fell into the Atlantic Ocean after the explosion. Recovery ships brought many of these pieces back for investigators. Some of the pieces sank to the bottom of the ocean. Other pieces floated away on the waves.

Two large pieces of *Challenger* washed up on shore in Cocoa Beach, Florida, in 1996. These pieces had been in the ocean for about 10 years.

The Investigation

The U.S. government held an investigation after the *Challenger* disaster. Top scientists from around the country, including former astronauts Neil Armstrong and Sally Ride, took part in the investigation. They studied the video of the explosion. They looked at diagrams of the orbiter and the SRBs. They read all of the information NASA had on the launch.

Investigators quickly learned the cause of the disaster. The engineer who had called NASA the morning of the launch had been right. The cold temperatures had prevented some parts inside the SRBs from working properly.

This memorial to *Challenger*'s crew stands in Arlington National Cemetery in Virginia.

Challenger's problems began in the
solid-rocket boosters.

The O-Rings

Each of *Challenger's* SRBs was divided into four parts. The parts came together at complex joints. Each joint was sealed with two O-rings. These seals prevented hot gases from escaping through the joints.

The boosters' O-rings bend easily in warm weather. But in cold weather, they become stiff. The stiff O-rings could not properly seal the joints. Hot gases escaped through the joints and sprayed fire away from the boosters. The fire caused the external fuel tank to explode.

NASA officials knew that launching in cold temperatures could be dangerous, but they were under great pressure from the government to go ahead with the launch. They feared that delaying the launch again would look like a failure.

Learn About:

New safety measures

Improved O-rings

Emergency exits

What We Have Learned

Investigators found that cold temperatures caused the O-rings to fail, but they also knew that people had made many mistakes. NASA officials had not made safety their first concern. They also had shown poor communication. The engineers who could explain the dangers never got to talk to the highest NASA officials.

Changes

NASA spent more than two years studying the *Challenger* disaster. It did not launch any shuttles during this time. The next shuttle to launch was *Discovery* on September 29, 1988.

After the *Challenger* disaster, NASA made many changes to the shuttle program. Engineers designed new O-rings. They also added a third set of O-rings to each joint. NASA engineers test these O-rings and many other systems before each launch.

Challenger's crew compartment did not contain an emergency exit. All space shuttles now have an emergency exit in the crew compartment. Crew members slide down a chute that leads out of the orbiter. They carry parachutes that could help them return safely to Earth. This emergency exit is useful only when the space shuttle is in gliding flight within about 100,000 feet (30,000 meters) of the ground. It would not have helped the astronauts aboard *Challenger*.

NASA officials plan to send another teacher into space in 2004. Barbara Morgan, an elementary school teacher from Idaho, was

Christa McAuliffe's backup for the *Challenger* mission. In 1998, NASA began training Morgan to join another NASA mission. Unlike McAuliffe, Morgan is going through full astronaut training. She will be an astronaut instead of a participant-observer.

Discovery was the first space shuttle to launch after the *Challenger* disaster.

Timeline

NASA launches the first space shuttle, called *Columbia*.

Teacher Christa McAuliffe is selected as the first private citizen to join a space mission.

1974   **1981**   **1983**   **1985**

Workers begin to assemble the space shuttle that will become *Challenger*.

NASA launches the space shuttle *Challenger* for the first time.

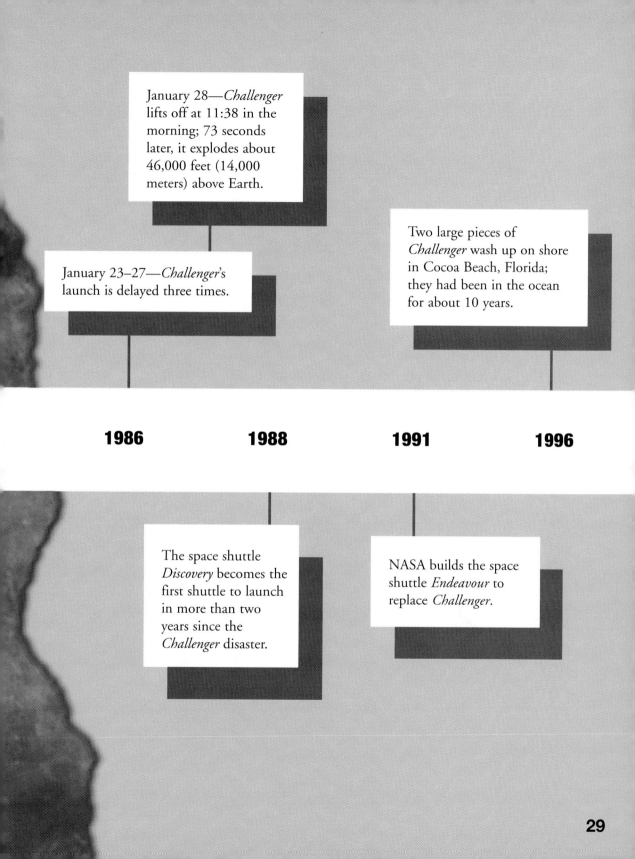

January 28—*Challenger* lifts off at 11:38 in the morning; 73 seconds later, it explodes about 46,000 feet (14,000 meters) above Earth.

January 23–27—*Challenger*'s launch is delayed three times.

Two large pieces of *Challenger* wash up on shore in Cocoa Beach, Florida; they had been in the ocean for about 10 years.

1986

1988

1991

1996

The space shuttle *Discovery* becomes the first shuttle to launch in more than two years since the *Challenger* disaster.

NASA builds the space shuttle *Endeavour* to replace *Challenger*.

Words to Know

altitude (AL-ti-tood)—the height of an object above the ground

cargo bay (KAR-goh BAY)—the area in a space shuttle orbiter where large equipment is carried

hydrogen (HYE-druh-juhn)—an element that combines with oxygen to produce a space shuttle's launching power

orbiter (OR-bit-ur)—the main part of a space shuttle; the orbiter is the part of the shuttle that goes into space and returns to Earth.

O-ring (OH-ring)—a rubber ring that seals the joints in solid-rocket boosters

oxygen (OK-suh-juhn)—an element that combines with hydrogen to produce a space shuttle's launching power

To Learn More

Bredeson, Carmen. *The Challenger Disaster: Tragic Space Flight.* American Disasters. Berkeley Heights, N.J.: Enslow, 1999.

DeAngelis, Gina. *The Apollo 1 and Challenger Disasters.* Great Disasters, Reforms and Ramifications. Philadelphia: Chelsea House, 2001.

Jeffrey, Laura S. *Christa McAuliffe: A Space Biography.* Countdown to Space. Springfield, N.J.: Enslow, 1998.

Useful Addresses

Challenger Center for Space Science Education
1250 North Pitt Street
Alexandria, VA 22314

Kennedy Space Center Visitor Complex
Mail Code: DNPS
Kennedy Space Center, FL 32899

Internet Sites

NASA
http://www.nasa.gov

NASA Human SpaceFlight
http://spaceflight.nasa.gov

U.S. Space Camp
http://www.spacecamp.com

Index